JESUS IS COMING...

ANY DAY
NOW

AMIR TSARFATI

HARVEST PROPHECY
AN IMPRINT OF HARVEST HOUSE PUBLISHERS

Cover design by Bryce Williamson

Cover photo © dwleindecker, GeorgePeters/Getty Images

Interior design by Chad Dougherty

For bulk, special sales, or ministry purchases, please call 1-800-547-8979. Email: Customerservice@hhpbooks.com

This logo is a federally registered trademark of the Hawkins Children's LLC. Harvest House Publishers, Inc., is the exclusive licensee of this trademark.

Any Day Now

Copyright © 2020 by Amir Tsarfati
Published by Harvest House Publishers
Eugene, Oregon 97408
www.harvesthousepublishers.com

ISBN 978-0-7369-8670-0 (pbk)
ISBN 978-0-7369-8667-0 (eBook)

Library of Congress Control Number: 2022931417

Printed in the United States of America

22 23 24 25 26 27 28 29 30 / BP / 10 9 8 7 6 5 4 3 2

CONTENTS

CHAPTER 1

ANY DAY NOW

Many mornings I'll wake up, pour myself a cup of coffee, then take my Bible out to my back porch. As I settle into a cushioned chair, I'll take in the beautiful scene below me. Stretched out for miles is fertile land colored by whatever bountiful crop has been sown in it. Often there is a light breeze that the predatory birds take full advantage of as they hunt their scurrying prey. Taking in this beauty, my first thought is often, *Coffee is the greatest proof that there is a Creator God*. But my second thought is how unbelievable it is that conceivably in less than a decade or two that whole valley below me will be filling up with the armies of many nations. These armies will unite to march south to destroy the city of Jerusalem.

You see, that beautiful panorama below my backyard is the Jezreel Valley, also known as the Valley of Megiddo, also known as the Valley of Armageddon. If I see those armies gathering together, that will alert me to the following: First, I know that Israel has already endured a devastating attack—likely nuclear in nature. I know that a great world leader has arisen, uniting the nations of the world. I know that earthquakes and famines and other natural disasters have devastated the earth. I know that in Jerusalem a new temple has been built. And I know that the Mount of Olives is ready to feel the feet of the returning Savior, who will come as the King of kings and Lord of lords.

I also know that I will not be around to see any of this taking place. If those armies are down there, then I'm not up here—sipping on my coffee, enjoying the view. I'll already be in heaven. I'll be in the presence of my Savior, having been snatched up by Him seven years previously. And I'll be preparing to return with Him to this earth one more time. So, if you're planning on still being around at the end of the great tribulation, I'll leave the keys under the front mat for you—it should be quite a view.

God is working out His plan. There will soon be a day when the church is taken up to meet Jesus in the air. There will come a time when God disciplines the people of Israel in a way that ultimately leads to their repentance. And there will come a day when those who have rejected the free gift of God's salvation will suffer His wrath because of their sins.

The *what* of this coming day isn't the primary question of this book. I dealt with the rapture and the Antichrist in great detail in my previous book, *The Last Hour*. While we will deal with some of the events of the tribulation in *The Day Approaching*, our main focus here will be on the *when*.

Now, it's time for me to come 100 percent clean with you. I have no clue as to the day and time of Christ's return. But I'm in good company. No person knows the day and time. The angels don't know. Not even the Son of God Himself knows. Jesus said, "Of that day and hour no one knows, not even the angels of heaven, but My Father only" (Matthew 24:36). The Father has got the timing planned out to the minute, but He's keeping His cards close to His chest. What I can tell you is that as I look at the events unfolding in the world around us, I firmly believe that the day of Jesus' return is rapidly approaching.

I don't know about you, but I can't wait for that day when I see Jesus. I think about it. I imagine what it will be like. I study the Scriptures to learn all I can about it. This longing to see my Savior is not only in my heart, but also on my lips. I believe that we should proclaim our desire for Jesus to come. The apostle John wrote in the book of Revelation, "The Spirit and the bride say, 'Come!' And let him who hears say, 'Come!'" (22:17). John himself expressed his own desire when he said, "Even so, come, Lord Jesus!" (verse 20). Have you asked Jesus to come? Have you expressed to Him your excitement at seeing Him and your desire to be with Him forever? Have you ever taken a moment to close your eyes and picture what it will be like?

Imagine sitting around the dinner table with your family. You're about to take your first bite of your wife's wonderful spaghetti bolognese when you feel something happening—a tingling, a lightness—and suddenly, you are airborne. As you and your family shoot upward, you barely have time to see the look of wonder on their faces when another face catches your full attention. You recognize it immediately, even though you've never seen it before. It is the face of Jesus in all His glory and majesty. All the pains, fears, worries, and sorrows of the world are left behind in your recently departed dining room. Only joy, peace, and happiness await you as you enter into eternity.

This is the rapture. It is not just a story. It is not a feel-good religious fairy tale. It is an actual event that will take place in real time in the real world. I must admit that as I travel around the globe, I am amazed at how many people in the churches that I visit don't believe in the rapture. Others, more than not believing in it, are hostile to the whole idea. They don't even want to hear it mentioned.

I was speaking to a pastor friend of mine not long ago who told me that rather than looking forward to the advent of Christ's rule on earth, he believes we are now living in the kingdom of God. He says that all the events described in Revelation took place by AD 70. When Rome destroyed the temple and slaughtered thousands of Jews, the wrath of God was sated. No more need for judgment; no more need for hell. Our satisfied Lord will eventually save everyone. I was shocked to hear the extent of this pastor's deception.

We are living in a time of great anticipation surrounding the soon return of Christ, but it is also a time of great apostasy. Many antichrists exist in the world, both outside of the church and inside. As believers, we must know the truth of God's plan for mankind and how we fit into it. It is out of this knowledge that we find our mission and our hope.

God Wants You to Know His Plan

The title of this chapter is "Any Day Now." If you have ever been on a tour with me, you will recognize this phrase immediately. I say these words probably 50 times a day to those who are casually finishing their cup of coffee or browsing for their next olive wood purchase while everyone else is waiting for them on the bus. It is often accompanied by an eye-roll or a wave of my watch. If these stragglers would have taken the time to look around, they would realize that they were the only members of the tour who weren't with the rest of the group.

If we take the time to look around us, we can't help but realize that there is a strong sense of Any Day Now in the world. It is so obvious to me, and I'm not the only one who feels it. In early 2017, the number of Google searches for "World War 3" hit its highest level ever. What precipitated this spike? The combination of President Donald Trump's escalation of activities in Syria and his dealings with North Korea.[1] Both of these situations have calmed since that moment of national panic, but there is still a sense that something significant is going on. Within us is a built-in curiosity about what is going to happen in the future, and a sense that the way the world is now must eventually come to an end.

Much of this curiosity stems from a fear of the unknown. Newspapers and 24-hour cable news channels are constantly bombarding readers and viewers with why they should be terrified if the US president does this or Iran does that or North Korea does something. Not long ago, a headline in *The Telegraph* read "World 'on the brink of thermo-nuclear war', as North Korea mulls test that could goad Trump."[2] Try getting a good night's sleep after reading that. People accuse Christians and the Bible of being doomsayers, but it's actually the media who are the doomsayers. In contrast, it's Christ and the Bible that give hope. It's Christ and the Bible that say, "Yes, eventually this world is going to blow apart. But let Me tell you how you can ensure yourself a flight out of here before it happens."

God wants you to know His plans—His plans for the world, for Israel, for the church, and for you. Are you interested in knowing the future? Then you need to go to the One who laid it out. He's already written what will happen; you just need to read it. Where should you start? All you need to know about what's coming was revealed through God's prophets.

These prophets were faithful yet tragic figures. The last thing anyone wanted to hear was God saying, "Guess what? I'm choosing you to be My prophet." The prophets were destined for a life of struggle, suffering, and pain. Yet nearly all raised their hands when God called. When the Lord asked, "Whom shall I send, and who will go for Us?," like Isaiah, they stepped up and said, "Here am I! Send me" (Isaiah 6:8).

These days, everybody wants to be a prophet. I guess it's because there is profit in being a prophet. I am not a prophet. I come from a nonprofit organization. Today's prophets teach their own opinions and call them words from the Lord. But man's opinion doesn't come close to meeting the biblical standard for prophecy. "No prophecy of Scripture is of any private interpretation, for prophecy never came by the will of man, but holy men of God spoke as they were moved by the Holy Spirit" (2 Peter 1:20-21). When Jeremiah and Isaiah and Hosea and Malachi and all the other prophets spoke prophetically, they were not speaking their own thoughts and viewpoints. Prophecy originates in the mind of God, and then is spoken through the mouths of His chosen messengers.

God's prophetic message—His plan for this world—has been revealed to us in the Bible. From Genesis to Revelation, the Lord lays out His blueprint for eternity step by step and piece by piece. Despite the fact He has given us 66 books of revelation, there are many who look only to the New Testament for their eternal guidance. They assume that the Old Testament was just fine for its time, but then Jesus came along and brought the New. The Old was great for the Jews, but we're the church. Who wants the Old when you can have the New and improved?

So much of what God wants us to know about the future is found in the distant past—before the church and the New Testament. If we limit ourselves to Matthew 24–25 and the book of Revelation, we will get only part of the story. In Hebrews, we read that "God, who at various times and in various ways spoke in time past to the fathers by the prophets, has in these last days spoken to us by His Son" (1:1-2). The God who spoke His truth through Jesus and the New Testament writers is the same God who pulled back the curtain on the end times through the Old Testament prophets.

When we read the words of Malachi or Zechariah or Hosea, we know they are from the mouth of the Lord. The prophet was just a spokesperson. He likely understood very little of what he saw and said. In fact, in many cases, today we understand much more than the prophets ever did about what God is going to do as He brings salvation to the church, discipline to the Jews, and wrath upon the earth. And so much of what we see in the prophets and the New Testament seems to indicate that this great Day of the Lord is coming closer and closer.

The Times Are Moving Forward

History is moving forward, and the events that are rapidly approaching can be separated into two categories: those we can do something about, and those we can't. Most future happenings fall into the latter category. When the angel Gabriel came to the prophet Daniel, he told him what was definitely going to happen. He said, "Seventy weeks are determined for your people and for your holy city" (Daniel 9:24). The events that Gabriel spoke of *will* take place—they've been determined. You can try to stop the works of God, but you won't get very far. Imagine a speeding train hurtling in your direction. It doesn't matter how earnestly you desire to stop it, that's not going to happen. You can brace your feet. You can grit your teeth. You can scream at the train with all your might, "Thou shalt not pass!" Still, within moments, the train will run right over you and you'll be flattened like a pita.

If the world's future is so much out of our control, does that mean we are utterly doomed? Is there anything we can do to give ourselves hope in God's grand plan? Most certainly. We can choose to follow Christ, giving ourselves to Him as our Lord and Savior. If we do that, then we are assured that when He returns for His church, we will be taken to Him.

However, if we choose to reject Him—or even if we simply ignore the choice, which is the same as turning our backs on Him—we will be left to experience the terrors of judgment. What a simple choice! Either we choose life eternal or we choose death. We will choose to escape the wrath of God, or we will choose to experience the tribulation and suffer for all eternity apart from our Creator. There is no other decision that we can make in our life that presents such a stark contrast. Praise the Lord that He has given us the opportunity to choose Him! But the day of choosing is now.

Why must it be now? Because the time left for making a choice may soon come to an end. As we keep our eyes on the news, it seems more and more as if the final days are nearly at hand. One key sign of the day approaching will take place in Syria. Isaiah prophesied that Damascus will one day be utterly annihilated: "Behold, Damascus will cease from being a city, and it will be a ruinous heap" (17:1). Up until recently, most people in the world had never even heard about Damascus. Those who did knew it as the "City of Jasmine," with a wonderful historical and modern culture. But now, as the center of the Syrian conflict, the city is on the front page of the newspapers almost daily. As hostilities not only continue but increase, it is not hard to envision the eventual leveling of that ancient city.

The times are moving forward. The Lord is shifting all the players into position and is setting up the playing field. Just one example of God's logistical work that would have been unheard of a mere decade ago relates to plans for a project under the Mediterranean Sea. This will be the longest underwater pipeline in the world, from Israel to Italy. This pipeline will carry natural gas from Israel's recently found gas fields to the European Union. Sounds wonderful, doesn't it? It does if you're not from Russia. What Putin and his cronies see is an upstart nation stealing their customers. Russia, whose economy is already shaky, can't afford to lose the European market, and they won't just sit by and watch their largest customer get taken away.

There are three truths that become evident as we observe current events. First, the events prophesied in the Word of God are taking shape all around us. The new ideas and plans of today's world leaders were known and talked about by God 2,800 years ago. There is no move that can be made that will take God off-guard. There is no strategy that can be implemented that He has not considered. King Solomon writes, "The king's heart is in the hand of the LORD, like the rivers of water; He turns it wherever He wishes" (Proverbs 21:1). When presidents and kings and prime ministers believe they are exercising their own great power and authority, they are actually following God's lead.

Second, there is a smoke screen of deception surrounding world events that is confusing many people. They are buying into the lies proclaimed by the media and politicians. An example of this fake news has to do with the chemical attacks by Syrian

President Bashar al-Assad upon his people. One group of people say, "Of course he did it. That's the kind of person he is." While others say, "How can you say such a thing? He would never do that to his people."

Even Christians get caught up in this kind of duplicity and fight amongst each other. Why? Is it so surprising that Syria would gas its own people? I'll let you in on a little secret if you promise to keep it just between us: I know the name of the Syrian pilot who dropped chemical bombs on his people. I know the name of his aircraft. The Israeli government knows his address and phone number. We know where he took off from, when he did it, and we have a video of him dropping the bombs. Yet Christians still argue over whether these kinds of things have happened. Why do we let Satan divide us over politics and opinions?

Still, in the midst of all the deception and division, we see tremendous acts of God's people showing His love. On Palm Sunday of 2017, there was a horrific attack in Egypt. ISIS targeted two Coptic churches, and the bomb blasts killed 47 and injured at least 109.[3] So many lives taken, so many bodies maimed. Yet how did the leaders of the Coptic church respond? Believe it or not, they thanked ISIS. You may wonder how that is possible after such an atrocity. First, they thanked the terrorists because they had sent 47 people into the arms of Jesus. In the moment of that blast, those who were killed saw their Savior face to face. Second, since that attack, their churches have been absolutely packed. All those who were lazy about coming to worship are now running to church.

As if thanking their enemies was not enough, the leaders of the Coptic church followed up by telling their ISIS attackers, "We love you." They told the extremists that they understood they are caught up in a lie and don't know the truth. Finally, the church leaders went one step further. They said, "And we commit to praying for you."[4] This put Jesus' words from the Sermon on the Mount into flesh: "Love your enemies, bless those who curse you, do good to those who hate you, and pray for those who spitefully use you and persecute you, that you may be sons of your Father in heaven" (Matthew 5:44-45). These brothers and sisters of the Coptic church showed themselves to be sons and daughters of their Father in heaven and ambassadors of the love of their Savior.

For those of us who are Christians, death has

truly lost its sting. Christ in us allows us to love our enemies and pray for those who would do us harm. This is because we can see the bigger picture. We have not become lost in the smoke screen of deception. We know that for us, "to live is Christ, and to die is gain" (Philippians 1:21). No longer should we be afraid of death. When our time comes, we can go happily into that dark night knowing that the light of eternal life awaits us.

The third truth we learn from observing current events is that God is revealing Himself to people all around the world. There are changes taking place in people's hearts and the gospel is finding its way into places never before reached. This is the direct hand of God at work. I receive hundreds of emails and messages every day from every corner of the globe—Malaysia, the Philippines, Japan, North America, Australia, South America, Israel, Europe. What so many of these people are writing is, "Amir, I'm having visions," or "Amir, I keep having these dreams." The prophet Joel wrote:

> It shall come to pass afterward
> that I will pour out My Spirit on all flesh;
> your sons and your daughters shall prophesy,

> your old men shall dream dreams,
> Your young men shall see visions.
> And also on My menservants and on My
> maidservants
> I will pour out My Spirit in those days
> (Joel 2:28-29).

These people who write to me say that God has spoken to them in a clear way, saying, "I am coming soon." People in China and Mexico and New Zealand are all hearing the same message independently from one another. God is moving. He is speaking. He is coming soon.

As we read the newspapers and watch the cable channels, a contrast becomes evident. On the one hand, everything seems to be falling apart. The talking heads will tell you nightly that we're all doomed and a nuclear holocaust is right around the corner. On the other hand, when we look through the lens of Scripture, everything is falling into place. The newspaper writers can't see it. They are trying to make sense of what's going on without having the capacity to understand. It's like small children trying to explain quantum physics—they simply don't have the capacity to do that. But when we look at world events through the lens of the Bible, we find the key to unlocking the truth.

"But wait," you may say, "the news and the Bible are two different things. The news is about now. The Bible is history and was written thousands of years ago." True, the Bible is history. But the Bible is also His story. It is the story of God's plan for this earth from the very beginning to the very end. In the pages of Scripture, you will find what was, what is, and what is yet to come. In fact, what you see happening in many of the nations today is right out of the Bible.

"Wait, Amir, are you going to tell me that Russia is in the Bible?" Yes! "Egypt and Ethiopia are in the Bible?" Yes and yes! "Iran and Turkey and Sudan?" Yes, yes, and yes! Much of what you see around you with the growing world powers and their alliances is straight out of the pages of biblical prophecy.

Ezekiel 38 tells us of the evil intentions of Russia when it describes how Ros will be led down to Israel as if a hook were put into its jaw. Ros will come down not for the purpose of peace, but plunder. Today, the Russians are the number one player in the Syrian civil war, and they don't even try to hide the fact that they are there primarily for the gas and oil. Russia's only warm-water seaport giving access to the

Mediterranean and the Middle East is in Syria. That's why Russia backs the government of Bashar al-Assad.

Who does Ezekiel say will be aligned with Ros? None other than Persia, which is modern-day Iran. The Iranians' goal is to be poised on Syria's border with Israel so that when the attack does come, they will be ready to pour into the Jewish state. Also in this Russian alliance are Sudan and Libya. The Russians have long had an interest in the oil fields of Libya and are looking for opportunities to put their nose under the Libyan tents. Oil, gas, Russia—it is no surprise to find them linked together again.

Standing with Israel against these enemies are Jordan and, through more recent and unofficial alliances, Saudi Arabia and Egypt. Surprisingly to many, the Saudis have signed a secret deal with Israel, saying, "If you want to attack Iran, feel free to use our airspace."[5] The Saudis did add a caveat promising that if Israel admitted to this alliance, they would deny it and condemn Israel in the UN. Is this secret alliance with Saudi Arabia spoken of in the Bible? No. But long before that region was called Saudi Arabia, it was called Sheba and Dedan. "Sheba, Dedan, the merchants of Tarshish, and all their young lions will say to you, 'Have you come to take plunder? Have you gathered your army to take booty, to carry away silver and gold, to take away livestock and goods, to take great plunder?'" (Ezekiel 38:13). Saudi Arabia will not join in the attack against Israel because they are allies. But neither will Saudi Arabia try to stop it. They will stand by ready to collect the spoils of what they assume will be a devastated nation.

And who is standing there next to the Saudis ready to scavenge? The merchants of Tarshish and all their young lions—Europe (the home of the city of Tarshish) and America (the ferocious young nation that was birthed out of Europe). Some 2,000, 3,000, even 4,000 years ago, God knew the identity of the players on today's political stage. Using the names of the countries in those times, He explained exactly what His future plans are.

The Signs of the Times

One day in the midst of all the crazy busyness of His ministry, Jesus took a break. He left the temple, went through a gate in the walls of Jerusalem, and walked up the Mount of Olives. There He sat by Himself and took in the view of the Holy City. Whether He was thinking or praying or just enjoying the silence, we don't know. What we do know is that

His private moment didn't last long. The disciples had been troubled by something that Jesus had just said to them at the temple. They had been oohing and aahing over the beauty of the temple, but rather than admiring the magnificent structure along with them, the Lord had said, "Do you not see all these things? Assuredly, I say to you, not one stone shall be left here upon another, that shall not be thrown down" (Matthew 24:2).

Troubled, the disciples approached Him for some answers. "Tell us, when will these things be? And what will be the sign of Your coming, and of the end of the age?" (verse 3).

Rather than rebuff them or plead His need for a little "Me" time, Jesus gave them an amazing answer. He told them that people would come seeking to deceive them and claim that Christ has returned. Wars and rumors of wars will have people shaking in their sandals, but the disciples were not to be afraid. "For nation will rise against nation, and kingdom against kingdom. And there will be famines, pestilences, and earthquakes in various places. All these are the beginning of sorrows" (verses 7-8). The world is going to get violent and dangerous, Jesus said, but that's just the beginning.

Look around the world today. Did Jesus just describe our time? Earthquake activity continues to increase. In just the last six years we have seen major volcanic eruptions from Mount Etna (Italy), Mount Sinabung (Indonesia), Mount Kelud (Indonesia), Mount Ontake (Japan), and Mount Calbuco (Chile). In 2018, Volcán de Fuego blew in Guatemala, killing 190 people. Later that same year, the infamous Anak Krakatoa in Indonesia erupted, which caused a tsunami that killed nearly 450 people and injured more than 14,000 more.[6] Famine continues to spread too. The UN has declared famine conditions in South Sudan, Yemen, Nigeria, and Somalia.[7] This desperate lack of food is not due to weather conditions but is mostly the result of rampant government corruption. All of what Jesus described exists today in our world, and in ever-increasing intensity.

How do you feel when you watch the news? Do you get nervous? Do you stay awake at night worrying? Let me tell you, there is no reason to stay awake. I live in a very safe country. However, I also live in a nation that is hated by most of the people who surround us. Many times I've had my day interrupted by an app on my phone that alerts me when rockets are fired from Gaza or the West Bank into Israel.

Imagine if rockets were regularly fired across your borders into your country. Despite that, I sleep like a baby every night. My peace comes from the fact that even if a rocket happened to break through our Iron Dome missile defense and land on the roof of my house, my family and I would wake up in the presence of our Savior. And in that coming time when Russia finally decides to take what belongs to Israel, it can drop all the bombs it wants on my house. My family and I won't be there. We'll be testing out our new bodies with the rest of the raptured church.

The news is bleak and the world is on a downward slide. The Bible says that when you begin to see these things take place, don't let your head droop down in sorrow. Instead, look up—your redemption is drawing near. Does that excite you? It should. Jesus is returning for His church, and we could meet Him in the clouds any day now.

CHAPTER 2

THE FIG TREE AND THE FINAL GENERATION

Not long ago, I was having dinner in the home of a friend in America. After the meal, all the dishes were taken into the kitchen and the familiar sounds of the post-dinner cleanup were heard. As my friend and I retired to his living room, the growl of the garbage disposal carried from the kitchen. "A week ago, you wouldn't have heard that sound," he said. Intrigued, I asked him to elaborate.

A week earlier, his disposal had jammed. This wasn't the first time, so he began his usual clear-the-disposal routine. First, he slid his hand through the sink drain to make sure nothing was blocking it. There wasn't. Second, he checked underneath the sink to make sure it was still plugged in. It was. Third, he retrieved a broom and used the broom handle to try to budge the blades. They were budge-less. The situation was beginning to seem hopeless as he stood there with his stinky hand holding a scarred broom. Defeated, he called a plumber.

Three hours later, the plumber arrived. Before he even looked at the disposal unit, he asked, "Did you press the reset button?"

"The what?"

The plumber opened the cabinet and knelt down, thankfully pulling up the back of his pants before he did so. He reached his hand around to the back of the unit, then stood up, turned on the water, and flipped the disposal switch. The machine whirred to life. That was how my friend learned that his garbage disposal had a reset button. It had only cost him three hours, a $120 charge, and all his male dignity.

For us to truly understand what the Lord is saying to us in the Gospels and the rest of the Bible, we need to press our own reset button. We bring so many traditions and presuppositions into our biblical interpretations that it is often difficult to just read the Bible as it is written. So before you read further, take your finger, rest it against the side of your head, and press firmly. There! You've just reset your brain. Now you can read on.

It's very important to understand that when Jesus came 2,000 years ago, He did so as a Jew to the Jewish people. You would be surprised how many people aren't aware of this fact. I take people on tours all around Israel, and they see churches built up on many of the historical sites. Sometimes they pull me aside and want to know which one Jesus attended. "Amir, was Jesus Catholic, Orthodox, or Anglican?" "None of the above," I answer, "because Jesus was one hundred percent a Jew."

When Jesus taught His Jewish disciples, much of the time He did so in Jerusalem—the capital of Israel. Jerusalem was the capital then, and it is the capital now, no matter what the rest of the world wants to say. In fact, it has been the capital of Israel ever since David made it so 3,000 years ago. So Jesus, as a Jew, taught Jews Jewish things. And the subjects the disciples asked about were also completely Jewish in nature—issues related to the temple, the Messiah, and the last days. The Gentiles weren't into that kind of stuff. What did they care about believing in one God, a strange temple that had no statue of a deity in it, sitting around and doing nothing one specific day of the week, and strange beliefs about the last days? But these were the very subjects the Jewish disciples wanted to learn about.

The Parable of the Fig Tree

In Matthew 24 and Luke 21, we read about Jesus taking His disciples up to the Mount of Olives, which overlooked the temple. It was a powerful sight, and the disciples got to thinking. They asked Jesus some questions of genuine importance, which He welcomed. Gathering them around, He took time to explain the events of that era and of the future.

Isn't it awesome how we can come to God searching for truth and He will never turn us away? James tells us that if a person is wrestling with an issue, "let him ask of God, who gives to all liberally and without reproach, and it will be given to him" (James 1:5). Whether we are facing a major life decision or we need help trying to figure out a difficult biblical passage, the Holy Spirit is there to guide us and reveal His truth to us.

Jesus answered the disciples' questions in a passage that has come to be known as the Olivet Discourse because it was given on the Mount of Olives. Found in Matthew 24, it can be divided into two parts: the future of Israel (Matthew 24:4-31), and the future of the church (Matthew 24:32-51). In the first portion, Jesus speaks to the disciples as Jews. In the second, He talks to them as members of the soon-to-be church.

Wedged in between those two significant passages is a short pause of sorts—a four-verse tangent that is both significant and remarkable. Here, Jesus tells a parable about a fig tree:

> Now learn this parable from the fig tree: When its branch has already become tender and puts forth leaves, you know that summer is near. So you also, when you see all these things, know that it is near—at the doors! Assuredly, I say to you, this generation will by no means pass away till all these things take place. Heaven and earth will pass away, but My words will by no means pass away (Matthew 24:32-35).

The first important point to recognize is that Jesus says this is a parable. This is not a horticulture lesson. This is not a farmer's almanac. Jesus is telling a story about something that represents something else.

He also says that when the fig tree starts sprouting, "you know" that it is almost summer. Those are important words. You are not just hoping for the summer or longing for the summer. There is no doubt that a sprouting tree means that spring is about to move off the scene and be replaced by warmer weather. Once more, Jesus says that when you "see" these signs, you will know that the time is near. You will not simply hear about the sprouting fig tree or think about it or maybe dream about it. You, with your own two eyes, will recognize these signs and know their implications.

Again, these verses serve as a transition between Jesus' message to the Jews and His message to the church. It is here that Jesus is shifting His conversation with the disciples, speaking to them first as the former and then as the latter. They are not just Jews, they are also part of the family of God.

When the church began, it was primarily Jewish. It took until Acts 15 and the Council at Jerusalem for the Jewish believers to figure out what to do with these Gentiles who had begun pouring in, eating their bacon and lobster rolls. Those of us who are Jewish believers must live in both worlds. Ethnically, I am Jewish, but Israel is not where my true citizenship belongs. As soon as I became a believer, my citizenship shifted—I received a new passport. "For our citizenship is in heaven, from which we also eagerly wait for the Savior, the Lord Jesus Christ, who will transform our lowly body that it may be conformed to His glorious body, according to the working by which He is able even to subdue all things to Himself" (Philippians 3:20-21).

Yes, we as Christians have an earthly citizenship, but our first loyalty is to the kingdom of God. We are just sojourners on this earth. When our time on earth is over, we are going to our true home.

How Long Is a Generation?

What is the purpose of the fig tree parable? It is to identify the generation that will not pass away before the world, as we know it, draws to a conclusion. That's pretty exciting when you stop to think about it. Imagine being part of that final generation that sees God's end game playing out. But what does it mean to be part of this generation that will not pass away? Before we can answer that question, we have an even more basic one to deal with: What is a generation? This may seem simple, but many have wrestled with the definition of this crucial word over the ages.

Some say that a generation equals the longevity of mankind. In other words, it is one human life-span long. While preaching in Pisidian Antioch, Paul equated the word "generation" with the length of David's life. He said, "David, after he had served his own generation by the will of God, fell asleep, was buried with his fathers, and saw corruption" (Acts 13:36). In this biblical context, a generation begins at conception and ends at death.

And yes, life does begin at conception. David the psalmist wrote, "Your eyes saw my substance, being yet unformed. And in Your book they all were written, the days fashioned for me, when as yet there were none of them" (Psalm 139:16). God's plan for every person begins even before they are formed in the womb. I know a man who went through fertilization treatments with his wife. Just prior to the procedure in which the fertilized eggs were placed into her womb, this soon-to-be father was brought to a microscope. There, he saw his daughter six days after conception. She was merely a little mass of cells. Now she's 18 years old and preparing for college. What he saw through that microscope was no less human—no less alive—than what he will soon see walk onto a stage to receive her high school diploma.

Biblically, there is no pro-life versus pro-choice debate. The opposite of pro-life is pro-death. That is what our world's abortion culture promotes. Moses, just before he died, called the people of Israel together and offered them a choice. "I call heaven and earth as witnesses today against you, that I have set before you life and death, blessing and cursing; therefore choose life, that both you and your descendants may live" (Deuteronomy 30:19). With God, the choice is always life.

According to the theory that a generation refers to the length of a person's life, a generation is equal to the average life span of a group of people living at about the same time. Before the biblical flood, the average life span of mankind was around 900 years. Can you imagine that? You meet someone on the street and ask him how old he is. "Oh, six hundred or so. It's hard to remember exactly after so long."

"Six hundred? I can't even remember my six hundreds, they were so long ago," you reply. "When we lit my last birthday cake, my house burned down."

I don't know about you, but I don't want to live that long in this body. I haven't even reached half a century in age, and I'm already tired of it. I'm ready for the incorruptible upgrade I'm going to get when Jesus returns.

A second option for determining the length of

a generation is by using what is called a "wilderness generation." This uses the length of the Hebrew wanderings in the wilderness as the definition. When the Israelites refused to trust God and enter the Promised Land, He swore an oath of punishment against them:

> "Surely none of the men who came up from Egypt, from twenty years old and above, shall see the land of which I swore to Abraham, Isaac, and Jacob, because they have not wholly followed Me, except Caleb the son of Jephunneh, the Kenizzite, and Joshua the son of Nun, for they have wholly followed the Lord." So the Lord's anger was aroused against Israel, and He made them wander in the wilderness forty years, until all the generation that had done evil in the sight of the Lord was gone (Numbers 32:11-13).

A 40-year period of time was required for the disobedient generation of Moses' day to die off in the wilderness.

However, those who hold to the 40-year generation concept do not take into account the total age of those who had sinned against the Lord. The curse was given against those who had reached 20 years of age and older. After the 40-year judgment period was completed, there were no men left beyond 60 years of age except Joshua and Caleb. So that would have to be the number used to determine the length of a generation—20 plus 40. But 20 was just the minimum. There could have been people who lived much longer. If someone was 50 when the judgment was pronounced, he or she could have lived all the way to age 90 before dying in the wilderness. Then there were also the outliers—Aaron died at age 123, Moses reached 120, Joshua was 110 when he died, and Caleb was somewhere past 85.

I believe the answer to the generational question lies in the Psalms. In Psalm 90 we find a special poem. It is the oldest psalm in the Bible, and it is the only one written by Moses. Here, this great prophet wrote, "All our days have passed away in Your wrath; we finish our years like a sigh. The days of our lives are seventy years; and if by reason of strength they are eighty years, yet their boast is only labor and sorrow; for it is soon cut off, and we fly away" (Psalm 90:9-10).

If ever there was doubt that Moses was a Jew, all one needs to do is to read this depressing passage. The two verses are one long groan. What's noteworthy here is the life span Moses lays out. Our days are 70 years, but if you're working out, watching your fat intake, and remembering your vitamins, then maybe you'll make it to 80. That is the length of a life.

This is similar to the life span theory we looked at earlier—Moses lays out a generation as being from birth to death. The early mega-year people who lived before the flood were outliers. The next time you are in church, look around, and you will likely see a generation of people. You will see some newborns and you will see some of the dear saints in their nineties. This is the length of a generation—somewhere between 70-100 years.

The Three Plants of Israel

Now that we've determined the length of a generation, we need to identify who this generation is that Jesus speaks of. There are some who suggest He was talking about the people who were alive during the time He spoke the parable. Others say that the generation refers to the people of Israel in their entirety. But neither one of those options works. The reason they don't is because of the identity of the tree. The fig tree that Jesus speaks of is Israel itself. Based on that fact, Jesus' generation could hardly say that the Israel of the first century was tender and putting forth leaves. Rather, they were under oppressive Roman rule. In fact, just four decades after Jesus told this parable, the Romans would wreak havoc upon Jerusalem and destroy the temple. The Jewish people themselves are also disqualified from being the generation. Remember, they are the fig tree. You can't both watch for the sign and be the sign.

"But, Amir," you say, "where does Jesus say that Israel is the fig tree?" He doesn't, but the prophets do. In the Bible, the nation of Israel is likened to three different plants—the vine, the olive tree, and the fig tree. The vine is the symbol of Israel's spiritual privileges. "You have brought a vine out of Egypt; you have cast out the nations, and planted it" (Psalm 80:8). Jesus, as a Jew, is not only part of the vine, but is Himself the true Vine. He says, "I am the vine, you are the branches. He who abides in Me, and I in him, bears much fruit; for without Me you can do nothing" (John 15:5). Jesus is the vine, and we who are in the church are the branches, which bear spiritual fruit. Thus, both Israel and the church have their identity closely connected to the vine.

The same is true with the olive tree: "I will be like the dew to Israel; he shall grow like the lily, and lengthen his roots like Lebanon. His branches shall spread; his beauty shall be like an olive tree, and his fragrance like Lebanon" (Hosea 14:5-6). This gnarled tree is a symbol of Israel's religious privileges. What a blessing it is for the church to be allowed to be grafted into the tree, sharing in the privileges given to Israel. "And if some of the branches were broken off, and you, being a wild olive tree, were grafted in among them, and with them became a partaker of the root and fatness of the olive tree, do not boast against the branches. But if you do boast, remember that you do not support the root, but the root supports you" (Romans 11:17-18).

Praise the Lord, those of you who are in the church are now partakers of the root and fatness of the olive tree. Abraham, the father of the Jews, is now your father also. The Old Testament is now your book too. The church is fully assimilated into all the traditions and writings of Jewish history. But Paul warned, "Don't let this go to your head, church folk. Remember, you were grafted into them, not the other way around."

It is a different story when we come to the fig tree. "I found Israel like grapes in the wilderness; I saw your fathers as the firstfruits on the fig tree in its first season" (Hosea 9:10). This tree is a symbol of Israel's national privileges, and, as such, the church has no part of it. There is no assimilating—no grafting in—because it is in the fig tree that we find the Jews' ownership over the land, their ownership over Jerusalem, and their return to the homeland. The church cannot *be* the fig tree; it can only *see* the fig tree.

There are so many in the church who want to be the fig tree—they want to be Jews. In one sense, I can understand that. Recently, a friend emailed me and said that his parents had taken a DNA test. When the results came back, his mother discovered that her father, whom she had never known, was fully Jewish. This made my friend one-quarter Jew. I responded, "Exciting discovery—that explains why you're so brilliant!" However, if you are one of those who wishes you were Jewish, let me suggest you point your aspirations in a different direction. All you need to do is look at a little history to realize that being a Jew isn't always all it's cracked up to be.

Besides, as a Gentile, you cannot be part of the fig tree or grafted into it. No matter how much you wish to be a Jew, you cannot be one. It is not in your genes. You may wish you were 6'4" and an NFL linebacker, but if both your parents were 5'3" it's not going to happen. Is that right or wrong? No, it just is. You can be part of the olive tree and the vine because they have to do with spiritual and religious privileges. But the fig tree is all about national privileges, and those privileges belong to the people of the Jewish nation.

If, as a Gentile, your desire is to be a Jew, then you are missing out on your vital role in God's plan. Paul says in Romans 11 that you are to help provoke the Jews to jealousy. So why are you being provoked to jealousy by them and wanting to be Jewish? Instead, the church should be showing Israel just how wonderful it is to have a close, personal relationship with God—the relationship that the Lord originally intended to have with them. What is the ultimate goal of stirring up that jealousy? According to Paul, it is to "save some of them. For if their being cast away is the reconciling of the world, what will their acceptance be but life from the dead?" (Romans 11:14-15).

If you love the Jewish people, then what better way is there to show it than by embracing your close church-relationship with the Savior of the world, and thereby fulfilling your part in God's plan to bring salvation to the Jews?

The Branch Puts Forth Leaves

Back to the fig tree—since this is a parable, we understand that Jesus is not really talking about the fig tree. Instead, He is referring to the nation represented by the fig tree. He says, "Sure, they will be scattered and near death. They will be hated and surrounded by their enemies. The land itself will become desolate and barren. But there will come a generation that will see the resurrection of this nation represented by the fig tree."

Historically, this is exactly what happened to Israel. The desolation of the Promised Land began with the Roman siege of Jerusalem and the destruction of the temple in AD 70. It was solidified when Julius Severus, under orders from the Emperor Hadrian, put down the Bar Kokhba revolt in AD 135. Jerusalem was renamed Aelia Capitolina, and Judea became Syria Palestina. These events began the rapid decline of the land that was once marveled over by foreign dignitaries during the time of King David and King Solomon.

At the beginning of the twentieth century, Judea was still a dry wasteland, occasionally relieved by marshy and malarial swamplands. Yet God promised that would change. All it took for the land to be restored was God's own words.

You, O mountains of Israel, you shall shoot forth your branches and yield your fruit to My people Israel, for they are about to come. For indeed I am for you, and I will turn to you, and you shall be tilled and sown. I will multiply men upon you, all the house of Israel, all of it; and the cities shall be inhabited and the ruins rebuilt. I will multiply upon you man and beast; and they shall increase and bear young; I will make you inhabited as in former times, and do better for you than at your beginnings. Then you shall know that I am the LORD. Yes, I will cause men to walk on you, My people Israel; they shall take possession of you, and you shall be their inheritance; no more shall you bereave them of children (Ezekiel 36:8-12).

God spoke, and the dead land came alive. This barren wasteland now exports fruits and vegetables to the whole world. This is evidence of the amazing power of God's Word.

But there is more to the budding of the fig tree. Not only did God revitalize the land, but the nation was reborn. In Ezekiel 37, God's chosen people are pictured as a valley of dry, lifeless bones. If you have ever seen pictures of the survivors of the Holocaust when they were first given their freedom, it is easy to visualize the dry, dead bones metaphor. In Ezekiel, God told the prophet to prophesy,

> Behold, O My people, I will open your graves and cause you to come up from your graves, and bring you into the land of Israel. Then you shall know that I am the LORD, when I have opened your graves, O My people, and brought you up from your graves. I will put My Spirit in you, and you shall live, and I will place you in your own land. Then you shall know that I, the LORD, have spoken it and performed it (Ezekiel 37:12-14).

Again, God spoke, and this time the people came alive. God said, "Not only will I give you life, but I will give you life on your own soil." There is not a person on earth who has a rational explanation for how the Jews found their way back to their land and, in 70 short years, turned it into a world powerhouse.

Wait a minute—did you catch what I said about

70 short years? In May of 2018, Israel celebrated 70 years of nationhood. How long is a generation? Seventy to 100 years.

I'm going to assume that all of you who are currently reading this book are, at the present time, alive. This means you are part of the generation that sees Israel back in the land. You are alive to see the nation flourish. You have seen this miraculous work of God. Depending on your age, your great-grandparents or great-great-grandparents didn't see that coming. In fact, for them, the restoration of Israel would have seemed a laughable impossibility. Yet here it is—Israel's rebirth a reality in our generation.

For the first time ever, we have the church and Israel living and thriving at the same time. When the church was born in the first century, both Israel and the church were struggling. Then for many years, the church was strong, but Israel was scattered. That's why many people in the church began to worry that the prophecies about the nation of Israel would never come to fulfillment. They decided to help God out by saying, "We're the new Israel." No, you're not. Stay in your lane. The church is the church, and Israel is Israel. While the church thrived and the Jews struggled, God bided His time, saying, "Just wait and watch what I'm going to do with My people Israel. When I'm ready, My church is going to see My nation sprout and leaf. Then they'll know that they had better start looking up toward the skies."

We are the generation that has seen this sign.

A Rock-Solid Nonprediction

Fear not. Although I can tell you that I firmly believe that we are in the final generation, I will make no attempt to predict a date when the Lord will return. As we have seen, Jesus says, "Of that day and hour no one knows, not even the angels of heaven, but My Father only" (Matthew 24:36). Unfortunately, there are many date-predictors out there who will come up with some formula or who will receive some "new revelation." Essentially, they are saying, "Bless Your heart, Jesus. I'm sorry that You couldn't figure out the date, but I think I've got a little something that just might help You out a bit."

There's a good reason that Jesus didn't say, "I'm going to come and take you on October 27, 2030." It's because He wants you to be ready at all times. He wants you to live with expectancy. If Jesus had given us that date, then we would probably be living however we want, ignoring the kingdom of God, up until

October 26. Then we would all run around screaming out the gospel message, giving our possessions away to the poor, and spending our final evening on earth in an extended prayer meeting—all so that we could show Jesus how faithful we've been. In the parable of the ten virgins, Jesus said to "watch therefore, for you know neither the day nor the hour in which the Son of Man is coming" (Matthew 25:13). The Lord could come back at any moment. We need to be ready to meet our Savior.

Israel burst back onto the international scene as an independent nation on May 14, 1948. We are now in the optimal generational timeline from that date. We are not simply in the last days, we are in the last hour of the last days. As we saw in the previous chapter, the letter to the Hebrews begins, "God, who at various times and in various ways spoke in time past to the fathers by the prophets, has *in these last days* spoken to us by His Son, whom He has appointed heir of all things, through whom also He made the worlds" (Hebrews 1:1-2). Jesus came, and the last days began. The church has been waiting in expectancy since then.

Paul was convinced that Jesus could come and take him at any moment. When he was with the

Thessalonians, he told them, "Good news everyone— you're not going to die." Then he left, and some of them died. The ones who remained wrote to him and said, "Uh, Paul, we've got a problem." So Paul wrote back:

> I do not want you to be ignorant, brethren, concerning those who have fallen asleep, lest you sorrow as others who have no hope. For if we believe that Jesus died and rose again, even so God will bring with Him those who sleep in Jesus.
>
> For this we say to you by the word of the Lord, that we who are alive and remain until the coming of the Lord will by no means precede those who are asleep. For the Lord Himself will descend from heaven with a shout, with the voice of an archangel, and with the trumpet of God. And the dead in Christ will rise first. Then we who are alive and remain shall be caught up together with them in the clouds to meet the Lord in the air. And thus we shall always be with the Lord. Therefore comfort one another with these words (1 Thessalonians 4:13-18).

Paul didn't see the budding fig tree, yet he was still expectant. How much more anticipation should we feel as part of the generation that has seen the tender branches and the sprouting leaves? As we watch and wait, we must be about our Father's business. And when times get difficult, remember what Paul said in 1 Thessalonians 4:18 and comfort each other with his words.

CHAPTER 3

WHEN THE RESTRAINER STOPS RESTRAINING

The rain kept pouring down. It had been days since south-central Pennsylvania had seen the sun. The trickles ran down hills, forming streams that turned into small rivers, all looking for pools where the water could stop its journey and accumulate. One of those collection pools was Lake Conemaugh—a reservoir created when the South Fork Dam was built in the mid-nineteenth century. Now, decades later, the poor engineering of the dam was about to reveal itself in a disastrous way.

On May 31, 1889, the constant downpour finally prevailed. The South Fork Dam burst, sending 3.8 billion gallons of water crashing down the mountain toward unsuspecting Johnstown, Pennsylvania.

As the water rushed, it picked up debris—trees, cabins, railroad cars. It also swept up victims as it tore through helpless small towns—South Fork, Mineral Point, and East Conemaugh. When the flood finally reached Johnstown some 57 minutes later, the wall of water and wreckage was 35 feet high and traveling at 40 miles per hour. The destruction was unimaginable. A reported 2,209 people lost their lives that day, including 99 entire families wiped off the face of the earth.[8]

All that potential for destruction had been there for years, but it had been restrained by the dam. Once the restrainer was removed, devastation followed. This is the very picture that Paul presents in 2 Thessalonians 2. There is a restrainer in place right now, held secure by the Lord. But it will not remain there forever. A time is coming when the restrainer will be removed. On that day, people had better run for high ground, because devastation is about to pour down.

The Church's Role in Restraining

In the Sermon on the Mount, Jesus said, "You are the salt of the earth; but if the salt loses its flavor, how shall it be seasoned? It is then good for nothing but to be thrown out and trampled underfoot by men"

(Matthew 5:13). What does salt do? It slows down decay. This is our role on the earth. The only reason the world has not fallen completely into sin and ultimate judgment is because we are here to slow down the decline. If the church doesn't do its part in this world, then what good are we? We must intentionally be Christ to the people around us, restraining the judgment of God as He allows us.

Believers are the face of God to this world. Jesus said, "If you had known Me, you would have known My Father also; and from now on you know Him and have seen Him" (John 14:7). You don't have to be the Father to show people the Father. God is not in temples made by men; God is in men made to be His temple.

Paul, as he stood before the intellectual elite in Athens, said, "God, who made the world and everything in it, since He is Lord of heaven and earth, does not dwell in temples made with hands. Nor is He worshiped with men's hands, as though He needed anything, since He gives to all life, breath, and all things" (Acts 17:24-25). God is not in temples made by human hands; He is in temples that are made by His hands. Paul wrote to the Corinthians, "Do you not know that your body is the temple of the Holy

Spirit who is in you, whom you have from God, and you are not your own?" (1 Corinthians 6:19). We are the temples in which He dwells. So when the world sees us, they see Jesus. And when they see Jesus, they see the Father.

Our very presence in this world is what restrains the judgment that is yet to come. "Beloved, do not forget this one thing, that with the Lord one day is as a thousand years, and a thousand years as one day. The Lord is not slack concerning His promise, as some count slackness, but is longsuffering toward us, not willing that any should perish but that all should come to repentance" (2 Peter 3:8-9). We remain on this earth because the Lord is long-suffering. That's the God we serve. That's the God we love.

Paul wrote to Timothy that we should pray for all those in authority over us so that we may lead quiet, peaceable lives (1 Timothy 2:1-2). He then said, "This is good and acceptable in the sight of God our Savior, who desires all men to be saved and to come to the knowledge of the truth" (verses 3-4). God desires that all come to salvation, but this is utterly their choice. He has offered the free gift, but it must be accepted to be of any use.

If you haven't yet, receive the gift. That's all God

is asking of you. Accept Jesus as your Savior and Lord—make Him number one in your life. It's that simple. God wants you to be part of His family, and He wants *you* to want to be part of His family. He could have forced or coerced or tricked you. Instead, He straightforwardly put out the option. Choose God and receive life; reject God and receive death.

As long as the restrainer—God in us—remains in this world, the option is still open for those who have not received Him. However, as 2 Thessalonians tells us, there will come a day when the restrainer is removed. During the tribulation, few will search for the Lord because deceit from Satan will be so prevalent. Now is the day of our salvation. Today, before it is too late.

The Removal of the Restrainer

We have seen what the restrainer is—God's presence in the church. We have also seen what the restrainer is holding back—the Lord's judgment upon the world. When the church is removed, there will be nothing left to hold back the powerful, evil force of the enemy.

How will the restrainer be removed? We've already seen the answer to this question in 1 Thessalonians:

> The Lord Himself will descend from heaven with a shout, with the voice of an archangel, and with the trumpet of God. And the dead in Christ will rise first. Then we who are alive and remain shall be caught up together with them in the clouds to meet the Lord in the air. And thus we shall always be with the Lord. Therefore comfort one another with these words (4:16-18).

God will physically remove the restrainer from the earth. Once the Lord raptures His church to be with Him in the air, this will usher in the next phase of God's plan.

If the church is such a moderating presence—holding back the wrath of God as we shine the light of Christ—then why would the Lord want to remove us? Why doesn't He just extend His patience with the world by keeping us here? Because judgment must come. There is a soon-coming moment when the spiritual clock hands will reach 12:00 and the alarm will go off. In 2 Peter 3:8-9, we saw that the Lord is long-suffering, not wanting anyone to perish. What a wonderful show of God's grace! Yet notice the first word in verse 10—"but."

> But the day of the Lord will come as a thief
> in the night, in which the heavens will pass
> away with a great noise, and the elements
> will melt with fervent heat; both the earth
> and the works that are in it will be burned
> up (2 Peter 3:10).

The Lord is patient, but a time will come when His patience ends and judgment falls.

Mankind deserves the penalty that is soon approaching, yet even in the midst of pouring out judgment, the Lord will still be at work drawing people to Himself. God has a higher purpose for the tribulation—a purpose that runs beyond punishment. That horrible time of testing is specifically designed for Israel's salvation.

"But, Amir, is God really going to cause so much havoc just so Israel can be saved?" Through the prophet Hosea, the Lord said, "I will return again to My place till they acknowledge their offense. Then they will seek My face; in their affliction they will earnestly seek Me" (5:15). How sad it is that we tend to seek God only when things are at their worst. When life is going well, we tend to go about our business and ignore the God who gave our circumstances their present "okay-ness." Frequently it is pain that gets us to turn our eyes up to God. It takes affliction for us to drop to our knees before Him.

Reading the Signs

On that day when the restrainer is removed, God will usher in His wrath upon sinful mankind. Yet He will also use the judgments of the tribulation to get His chosen people to return to Him.

This brings us to the final question: When will the restrainer be removed? According to 2 Thessalonians 2, just before the Antichrist is revealed. When we see the signs of the Antichrist's rise all around us, then the rapture of the church is imminent. And when the church is raptured, the restrainer will be taken from this world.

What do today's signs tell us? Can we expect that the Antichrist will be revealed soon?

The answer is an emphatic *yes*.

Any Day Now

The Day is approaching. This is the Day when Jesus will rapture His church from the earth to meet Him. This is the Day of the Lord's judgment on sinners and the discipline of His people, Israel. This is the Day when Jesus will set foot upon the Mount of Olives, coming a second time to dwell on earth with His creation. This is the Day of the rule of the King of kings from His throne in Jerusalem. This is the Day of Satan's confinement, and of his eventual release and mankind's final rebellion. This is the Day of the Great White Throne judgment, when the sheep and the goats will be separated. And it is the Day of the new heaven and new earth, where we will enjoy the presence of the Lord forever.

Until that Day comes, let us rest in the hope of salvation through Jesus Christ. And let us be about our Father's business, knowing that our time is short. As Hebrews 10:23-25 says,

> Let us hold fast the confession of our hope without wavering, for He who promised is faithful. And let us consider one another in order to stir up love and good works, not forsaking the assembling of ourselves together, as is the manner of some, but exhorting one another, and so much the more as you see the Day approaching.

NOTES

1. Brooke Seipel, "Google Searches Spike for 'World War 3' amid Heightened Tensions Abroad," *The Hill*, April 14, 2017, https://the hill.com/blogs/blog-briefing-room/news/328948-google-searches-spike-for-world-war-3-amid-heightened-tensions.

2. Neil Connor and David Millward "World 'on the Brink of Thermo-Nuclear War', as North Korea Mulls Test That Could Goad Trump," *The Telegraph*, April 14, 2017, www.telegraph.co.uk/news/2017/04/13/us-may-launch-strike-north-korea-goes-nuclear-weapons-test/.

3. Dahlia Kholaif and Tamera El-Ghobashy, "Blasts Hit Two Egyptian Churches, Killing at Least 47," *The Wall Street Journal*, April 9, 2017, www.wsj.com/articles/egyptian-church-hit-by-bomb-blast-1491727099.

4. James Macintyre, "Egyptian Coptic Priest Delivers Inspiring Christian Message to Bombers: 'Thank You, We Are Praying for You,'" *Christian News on Christian Today*, April 13, 2017, www.christiantoday.com/article/egyptian-coptic-priest-delivers-inspiring-christian-message-to-bombers-thank-you-we-are-praying-for-you/107295.htm.

5. Avi Lewis, "Saudis 'Would Let Israeli Jets Use Their Air Space to Attack Iran,'" *The Times of Israel*, February 25, 2015, www.timesofisrael.com/saudis-said-to-mull-air-passage-for-israeli-jets-to-attack-iran/.

6. "List of Large Volcanic Eruptions in the 21st Century," Wikipedia, Wikimedia Foundation, May 9, 2019, https://en.wikipedia.org/wiki/List_of_large_volcanic_eruptions_in_the_21st_century.

7. "UN Issues Urgent Appeal for $4.4 Billion in Famine Aid," *Philanthropy News Digest*, March 14, 2017, http://philanthropynewsdigest.org/news/un-issues-urgent-appeal-for-4.4-billion-in-famine-aid.

8. "Facts About the 1889 Flood," *Johnstown Area Heritage Association*, www.jaha.org/attractions/johnstown-flood-museum/flood-history/facts-about-the-1889-flood/.

IF YOU WOULD LIKE TO READ MORE...

Any Day Now is an excerpt from Amir Tsarfati's book *The Day Approaching*. As you read, you'll learn about the

- plans God has for the world, Israel, and the church
- signs around us pointing to Christ's imminent return
- worldly deceptions that tempt people away from God's truth
- incredible work the Holy Spirit is doing in the world right now
- wonders that await every Christian in Jesus' kingdom

Amir's distinct perspective weaves biblical history, current events, and Bible prophecy together to illuminate the many mysteries about the end times.

ABOUT THE AUTHOR

Amir Tsarfati is a native Israeli and former major in the Israeli Defense Forces. He is the founder and president of Behold Israel—a nonprofit ministry that provides Bible teaching through tours, conferences, and social media. It also provides unique access to news and information about Israel from a biblical and prophetic standpoint. Amir is married with four children and resides in northern Israel.